POEMS FOR 10 YEAR OLDS

Susie Gibbs has worked in the world of children's poetry for eleven years. Her many nephews, nieces and godchildren were invaluable testing grounds for *Poems for 10 Year Olds*, and she very much hopes that they and their friends will enjoy this book. Susie lives aboard her narrowboat, *Hesperus II*, with one husband, no pets but plenty of wildlife.

Anna C. Leplar has illustrated numerous children's books, both in England and in Iceland where she lives with her family.

Also available from Macmillan Children's Books

POEMS FOR 7 YEAR OLDS
Chosen by Susie Gibbs

POEMS FOR 8 YEAR OLDS
Chosen by Susie Gibbs

POEMS FOR 9 YEAR OLDS
Chosen by Susie Gibbs

READ ME 1
A Poem for Every Day of the Year
Chosen by Gaby Morgan

UNZIP YOUR LIPS!
100 poems to read out loud
Chosen by Paul Cookson

ANOTHER DAY ON YOUR FOOT AND I WOULD HAVE DIED
Poems by John Agard, Wendy Cope, Roger McGough, Adrian Mitchell and Brian Patten

POEMS FOR 10 YEAR OLDS

CHOSEN BY
Susie Gibbs

ILLUSTRATED BY
Anna C. Leplar

MACMILLAN CHILDREN'S BOOKS

Dedicated with love to all my godchildren
Rufus, Harry, George, Clare, George and Anoushka.

First published 2000
by Macmillan Children's Books
a division of Pan Macmillan Limited
20 New Wharf Road, London, N1 9RR
Basingstoke and Oxford
www.panmacmillan.com

Associated companies throughout the world

ISBN 0 330 39209 3

3 5 7 9 8 6 4 2

A CIP catalogue record for this book is available from the British Library.

Printed by Mackays of Chatham plc, Chatham, Kent.

Contents

Ready Salted

Nothing else happened
That day.

Nothing much, anyway.

I got up, went to school,
Did the usual stuff.

Came home, watched telly,
Did the usual stuff.

Nothing else happened
That day.

Nothing much, anyway,

But the eyeball in the crisps
Was enough.

Ian McMillan

Poetic Thought

Oh Moon! When I look on thy beautiful face,
Careering along through the boundaries of space,
The thought has quite frequently come to my mind,
If ever I'll gaze on thy glorious behind.

Anon

Said to have been written by Edmund Gosse's serving maid, found in her mattress after her death.

Bug in a Jug

Curious fly,
Vinegar jug,
Slippery edge,
Pickled bug.

Anon

Toot! Toot!

A peanut sat on a railroad track,
His heart was all a-flutter;
The five-fifteen came rushing by –
Toot! Toot! Peanut butter!

Anon

A Student's Prayer

Now I lay me down to rest,
I pray I pass tomorrow's test.
If I should die before I wake,
That's one less test I'll have to take.

Anon

Two Dead Men . . . Such Nonsense!

One fine day in the middle of the night
Two dead men got up to fight.
Back to back they faced each other,
Drew their swords and shot each other.

Anon

The Sleepy Goalie

He shoots – he scores!
He yawns – he snores!

The goalie's fallen asleep again
On his face; a sloppy grin,
He's dreaming of saving the save of saves,
Behaving like a goalie should behave.

The crowd's in a frenzy, it's cup-final day,
But the goalie's let in five balls at the start of play,
He's fast asleep, curled up inside the net
He's sucking his thumb, he's not waking yet.

Seconds into the second half, he's tossing and turning,
He wouldn't wake now, even if the net was burning,
The other side are shooting goals like bullets from a
gun,
The final whistle blows. The score? 150 – 1.

Long after the players have left the ground
And the supporters have gone home,
The goalie's still there – a snoozy figure, all alone.
He'll be there till the next match, he never stops
dreaming,
Of the ball, the net, the crowd with their screaming.

He shoots – he scores!
He yawns – he snores!

Simon Pitt

Death of a Snowman

I was awake all night,
Big as a polar bear,
Strong and firm and white.
The tall black hat I wear
Was draped with ermine fur.
I felt so fit and well
Till the world began to stir
And the morning sun swell.
I was tired, began to yawn;
At noon in the humming sun
I caught a severe warm;
My nose began to run.
My hat grew black and fell,
Was followed by my grey head.
There was no funeral bell,
But by teatime I was dead.

Vernon Scannell

Until I Saw the Sea

Until I saw the sea
I did not know
that wind
could wrinkle water so.

I never knew
that sun
could splinter a whole sea of blue.

Nor
did I know before,
a sea breathes in and out
upon a shore.

Lilian Moore

I Asked the Little Boy who Cannot See

I asked the little boy who cannot see,
'And what is colour like?'
'Why, green,' said he,
'Is like the rustle when the wind blows through
The forest; running water, that is blue;
And red is like a trumpet sound; and pink
Is like the smell of roses; and I think
That purple must be like a thunderstorm;
And yellow is like something soft and warm;
And white is a pleasant stillness when you lie
And dream.'

Anon

The Word Party

Loving words clutch crimson roses,
Rude words sniff and pick their noses,
Sly words come dressed up as foxes,
Short words stand on cardboard boxes,
Common words tell jokes and gabble,
Complicated words play Scrabble,
Swear words stamp around and shout,
Hard words stare each other out,
Foreign words look lost and shrug,
Careless words trip on the rug,
Long words slouch with stooping shoulders,
Code words carry secret folders,
Silly words flick rubber bands,
Hyphenated words hold hands,
Strong words show off, bending metal,
Sweet words call each other 'petal',
Small words yawn and suck their thumbs
Till at last the morning comes.
Kind words give out farewell posies . . .

Snap! The dictionary closes.

Richard Edwards

The Toothless Wonder

Last night when I was sound asleep,
My little brother Keith
Tiptoed into my bedroom
And pulled out all my teeth.

You'd think that I would be upset
And jump and spit and swear.
You'd think that I would tackle Keith
And pull out all his hair.

But no! I'm glad he did it.
So what if people stare.
Now, thanks to the Tooth Fairy,
I'll be a millionaire!

Phil Bolsta

Peter Piper

Peter Piper picked a peck of
pickled peppers;
A peck of pickled peppers Peter
Piper picked.
If Peter Piper picked a peck of
pickled peppers,
Where's the peck of pickled peppers
Peter Piper picked?

Anon

A Poem With Two Lauras In It

'Laura. Is that you?'
'Yes, Laura. It's me.'
'Where are we?'
'We're caught inside some sort of
three verse poem.'
'POEM!'
'Look out. Here comes the second verse.
Jump!'

'Made it.'
'Now that we're in this poem, what do we do?'
'Maybe we should rhyme for a bit.'
'We'd have to find the words to fit.'
'Good. That worked. Think of something, Laura.'
'My jumper. It's made from angora.'
'Phew. Lucky you weren't wearing your sweatshirt.'
'Mum wouldn't let me. It was covered with dirt.'
'I wish this verse would come to an end.'
'This rhyming is driving me round the bend.'
'Look below you. It's verse number three.'
'I'll go first. You follow me.'

'That was a near thing. I'm exhausted.'
'Me too. Let's rest on this long line until the poem comes
to an end.'

John Coldwell

As the Witch Said to the Skeleton

WITCH: 'Come on out of that cupboard.'
SKELETON: 'I can't. I haven't got the face to.'

WITCH: 'Oh, come on. There's a dance down the road. Why don't you go?'
SKELETON: 'I haven't got any body to go with.'

WITCH: 'Don't you know *anyone*?'
SKELETON: 'No, I haven't got a single ghoul-friend.'

WITCH: 'Well, you needn't sound sorry for yourself.'
SKELETON: 'Well, I've lost my voice; among other things I haven't got a leg to stand on.'

WITCH: 'I suppose you were trying to throw
yourself off that cliff yesterday?'
SKELETON: 'No, I hadn't got the guts.'

WITCH: 'Scared, eh?'
SKELETON: 'Me scared? You couldn't make *me* jump
out of my skin, if you tried.'

WITCH: 'I don't know why I bother with you –
you're just a bone-idle old bonehead.'
SKELETON: 'That's right.'

Anon

The Painting Lesson

'What's THAT, dear?'
asked the new teacher.

'It's Mummy,' I replied.

'But mums aren't green and orange!
You really haven't TRIED.
You don't just paint in SPLODGES
– You're old enough to know
– You need to THINK before you work . . .
– Now – have another go.'

She helped me draw two arms and legs,
A face with sickly smile,
A rounded body, dark brown hair,
A hat – and, in a while,
She stood back (with her face bright pink):
'That's SO much better – don't you think?'

But she turned white
At ten to three
When an orange-green blob
Collected me.

'Hi, Mum!'

Trevor Harvey

Lone Mission

On evenings, after cocoa
(blackout down and sealed)
I would build plasticine Hamburgs
on green lino
and bomb them with encyclopaedias
(dropped from ceiling level)
from my Lancaster Bomber
built
(usually)
from table, box and curtains
turret made of chairs
radio and gas masks
tray and kitchenware
But:
Aircrew were my problem
gunners mid and rear
radio and bomber
nav. and engineer.

Each night I flew lone missions
through flack both hot and wild
and learnt it wasn't easy
to be an only child.

Peter Dixon

The Want-Want Twins

We are the Want-Want Twins.
We go from shop to shop.
We are the Want-Want Twins.
We don't know how to stop.
One day it's a bow and arrow.
Another it's a dinosaur.
What are we going to get tomorrow?
More. More. More.

We are the Want-Want Twins.
Our eyes sharp shiny pins.
Our hands quick shark's fins.
We go from shop to shop.
One day it's the game *Frustration.*
We don't know what we need.
Another it is compensation.
Greed. Greed. Greed.

We are the Want-Want Twins.
We're completely over the top.
We are the Want-Want Twins.
We don't know how to stop.
We send our parents every night
A list that goes like this:
2 new bikes. Don't be tight.
X.X.X.

We are the Want-Want Twins.
Money grows on trees.
We are the Want-Want Twins.
We are the bee's knees.
All we want is everything.
We don't know how to stop.
We will be the Want-Want Twins till we

drop

    drop

        drop.

Jackie Kay

A Date with Spring

Got a date with Spring
Got to look me best.
Of all the trees
I'll be the smartest dressed.

Perfumed breeze
behind me ear.
Pollen accessories
all in place.
Raindrop moisturizer
for me face.
Sunlight tints
to spruce up the hair.

What's the good of being a tree
if you can't flaunt your beauty?

Winter, I was naked.
Exposed as can be.
Me wardrobe took off
with the wind.
Life was a frosty slumber.
Now, Spring, here I come.
Can't wait to slip in
to me little green number.

John Agard

The Seagull

All day long o'er the ocean I fly,
My white wings beating fast through the sky,
I hunt fishes all down the bay
And ride on rocking billows in play.

All night long in my rock home I rest,
Away up on a cliff is my nest,
The waves murmur, murmur below,
And winds fresh from the sea o'er me blow.

Gaelic Folk Song

2 Poems about 4 Eyes

They call me Specky Four Eyes.
I wear glasses, so it's true,
I can see quite well why you're teasing me,
I've got two more eyes than you.

My spectacles are magical
for when you taunt and jeer,
I only have to take them off
to make you disappear.

Lindsay MacRae

The Pessimist

Nothing to do but work,
Nothing to eat but food,
Nothing to wear but clothes,
To keep one from going nude.

Nothing to breathe but air,
Quick as a flash 'tis gone;
Nowhere to fall but off,
Nowhere to stand but on.

Nothing to comb but hair,
Nowhere to sleep but in bed,
Nothing to weep but tears,
Nothing to bury but dead.

Nothing to sing but songs,
Ah, well, alas! alack!
Nowhere to go but out,
Nowhere to come but back.

Nothing to see but sights,
Nothing to quench but thirst,
Nothing to have but what we've got.
Thus through life we are cursed.

Nothing to strike but a gait;
Everything moves that goes.
Nothing at all but common sense
Can ever withstand these woes.

B. J. King

I Want to Be Monday

'I want to be Monday,' said Friday.
'It's such a dull spot that I've got.
I'd much rather have it than my day
That comes almost last of the lot.'

'What nonsense!' said Tuesday to Thursday.
'I don't think she knows what she's at.
There's no telling which is the worst day
Or which is the best, come to that.'

And Wednesday whispered to Sunday,
'I hope Monday doesn't say yes.
I've a feeling by changing the one day
We'll get in a terrible mess.'

Said Monday to Friday, 'A poor day?
But there's no one of whom we could speak
Who don't thank the stars that it's our day
At the end of a workaday week.'

'Of all the seven days,' declared Friday,
'I never thought I was the star!
If it's really that happy and high a day
I think I'll leave things as they are.
Yes, I think I'll leave things as they are.'

Charles Causley

Studup

'Owaryer?'
'Imokay.'
'Gladtwearit.'
'Howbowchew?'
'Reelygrate.'
'Binwaytinlong?'
'Longinuff.'
'Owlongubinear?'
'Boutanour.'
'Thinkeelturnup?'
'Aventaclue.'
'Dewfancyim?'
'Sortalykim.'
'Wantadrinkorsummat?'
'Thanksilestayabit.'
'Soocherself.'
'Seeyalater.'
'Byfernow.'

Barrie Wade

The Missing Sock

I found my sock
beneath the bed.
'Where have you been
all week?' I said.

'Hiding away,'
the sock replied.
'Another day on your foot
and I would have died!'

Roger McGough

The Dong with a Luminous Nose

When awful darkness and silence reign
Over the Great Gromboolian plain,
   Through the long, long wintry nights; –
When the angry breakers roar
As they beat on the rocky shore; –
   When Storm-clouds brood on the towering heights
Of the Hills of the Chankly Bore: –

Then, through the vast and gloomy dark,
There moves what seems a fiery spark,
   A lonely spark with silvery rays
   Piercing the coal-black night, –
   A Meteor strange and bright: –
Higher and thither the vision strays,
   A single lurid light.

Slowly it wanders, – pauses, – creeps, –
Anon it sparkles, – flashes and leaps;
And ever as onward it gleaming goes
A light on the Bong-tree stems it throws.
And those who watch at that midnight hour
From Hall or Terrace, or lofty Tower,
Cry, as the wild light passes along, –
      'The Dong! – the Dong!
   'The wandering Dong through the forest goes!
      'The Dong! the Dong!
   'The Dong with a luminous Nose!'

Long years ago
The Dong was happy and gay,
Till he fell in love with a Jumbly Girl
Who came to those shores one day,
For the Jumblies came in a sieve, they did, –
Landing at eve near the Zemmery Fidd
Where the Oblong Oysters grow,
And the rocks are smooth and grey.
And all the woods and the valleys rang
With the Chorus they daily and nightly sang, –
'Far and few, far and few,
Are the lands where the Jumblies live;
Their heads are green, and their hands are blue
And they went to sea in a sieve.'

Happily, happily passed those days!
While the cheerful Jumblies staid;
They danced in circlets all night long,
To the plaintive pipe of the lively Dong,
In moonlight, shine, or shade.
For day and night he was always there
By the side of the Jumbly Girl so fair,
With her sky-blue hands, and her sea-green hair.
Till the morning came of that hateful day
When the Jumblies sailed in their sieve away,
And the Dong was left on the cruel shore
Gazing – gazing for evermore, –
Ever keeping his weary eyes on
That pea-green sail on the far horizon, –
Singing the Jumbly Chorus still
As he sat all day on the grassy hill –

'Far and few, far and few,
Are the lands where the Jumblies live;
Their heads are green, and their hands are blue
And they went to sea in a sieve.'

But when the sun was low in the West,
The Dong arose and said; –
– 'What little sense I once possessed
'Has quite gone out of my head!' –
And since that day he wanders still
By lake and forest, marsh and hill,
Singing – 'O somewhere, in valley or plain
'Might I find my Jumbly Girl again!
'For ever I'll seek by lake and shore
'Till I find my Jumbly Girl once more!'

Playing a pipe with silvery squeaks,
Since then his Jumbly Girl he seeks,
And because by night he could not see,
He gathered the bark of the Twangum Tree
On the flowery plain that grows.
And he wove him a wondrous Nose, –
A Nose as strange as a Nose could be!
Of vast proportions and painted red,
And tied with cords to the back of his head.
– In a hollow rounded space it ended
With a luminous Lamp within suspended,
All fenced about
With a bandage stout
To prevent the wind from blowing it out; –
And with holes all round to send the light,
In gleaming rays on the dismal night.

And now each night, and all night long,
Over those plains still roams the Dong;
And above the wail of the Chimp and Snipe
You may hear the squeak of his plaintive pipe
While ever he seeks, but seeks in vain
To meet with his Jumbly Girl again;
Lonely and wild – all night he goes, –
The Dong with a luminous Nose!
And all who watch at the midnight hour,
From Halls or Terrace, or lofty Tower,
Cry, as they trace the Meteor bright,
Moving along through the dreary night, –
    'This is the hour when forth he goes,
    'The Dong with luminous Nose!
    'Yonder – over the plain he goes;
        'He goes!
        'He goes;
    'The Dong with a luminous Nose!'

Edward Lear

Mobile Home for Sale

Judy is a delightful
Mobile Home
with Central Heating
a warm Basement
superb Penthouse views
and includes luxury
Deep Pile Carpets
in black and white.
Fully Air-Conditioned
by large wagging tail.
This Border collie
would suit large family of fleas.

Roger Stevens

The Barkday Party

For my dog's birthday party
I dressed like a bear.
My friends came as lions
and tigers and wolves and monkeys.
At first, Runabout couldn't believe
the bear was really me. But
he became his old self again
when I fitted on his magician's top hat.
Runabout became the star, running about
jumping up on chairs and tables
barking at every question asked him.
Then, in their ordinary clothes,
my friend Brian and his dad arrived
with their boxer, Skip. And with us
knowing nothing about it, Brian's dad
mixed the dog's party meat and milk
with wine he brought. We started
singing. Runabout started to yelp
and the other six dogs joined –
yelping
Happy Barkday to you
Happy Barkday to you
Happy Barkday Runabout
Happy Barkday to you!

James Berry

The Lobster

'Tis the voice of the Lobster: I heard him
declare,
'You have baked me too brown, I must
sugar my hair.'
As a Duck with its eyelids so he with his
nose
Trims his belt and his buttons and turns
out his toes.

I passed by his garden and marked, with
one eye,
How the Owl and the Oyster were sharing
a pie;
While the Duck and the Dodo, the Lizard
and Cat,
Were swimming in milk round the brim
of a hat.

Lewis Carroll

The Hen

The Hen is a ferocious fowl,
She pecks you till she makes you howl.

And all the time she flaps her wings,
And says the most insulting things.

And when you try to take her eggs,
She bites large pieces from your legs.

The only safe way to get these,
Is to creep on your hands and knees.

In the meanwhile a friend must hide,
And jump out on the other side.

And then you snatch the eggs and run,
While she pursues the other one.

The difficulty is, to find
A trusty friend who will not mind.

Lord Alfred Douglas

The Visitor

A crumbling churchyard, the sea and the moon;
The waves had gouged out grave and bone;
A man was walking, late and alone . . .

He saw a skeleton on the ground;
A ring on a bony hand he found.

He ran home to his wife and gave her the ring.
'Oh, where did you get it?' He said not a thing.

'It's the loveliest ring in the world,' she said,
As it glowed on her finger. They skipped off to bed.

At midnight they woke. In the dark outside,
'Give me my ring!' a chill voice cried.

'What was that, William? What did it say?'
'Don't worry, my dear. It'll soon go away.'

'I'm coming!' A skeleton opened the door.
'Give me my ring!' It was crossing the floor.

'What was that, William? What did it say?'
'Don't worry, my dear. It'll soon go away.'

'I'm reaching you now! I'm climbing the bed.'
The wife pulled the sheet right over her head.

It was torn from her grasp and tossed in the air:
'I'll drag you out of bed by the hair!'

'What was that, William? What did it say?'
'Throw the ring through the window! THROW IT
AWAY!'

She threw it. The skeleton leapt from the sill,
Scooped up the ring and clattered downhill,
Fainter . . . and fainter . . . Then all was still.

Ian Serraillier

At the End of a School Day

It is the end of a school day
    and down the long drive
come bag-swinging, shouting children.
    Deafened, the sky winces.
    The sun gapes in surprise.

Suddenly the runners skid to a stop,
    stand still and stare
at a small hedgehog
    curled up on the tarmac
    like an old, frayed cricket ball.

A girl dumps her bag, tiptoes forward
    and gingerly, so gingerly
carries the creature
    to the safety of a shady hedge.
    Then steps back, watching.

Girl, children, sky and sun
    hold their breath.
There is a silence,
    a moment to remember
    on this warm afternoon in June.

Wes Magee

The Man Who Invented Football

The man who invented football,
He must have been dead clever,
He hadn't even a football shirt
Or any clothes whatever.

The man who invented soccer,
He hadn't even a *ball*
Or boots, but only his horny feet
And a bison's skull, that's all.

The man who invented football,
To whom our hats we doff,
Had only the sun for a yellow card
And death to send him off.

The cave-mouth was the goal-mouth,
The wind was the referee,
When the man who did it did it
In 30,000 BC!

Kit Wright

Haircut Rap

Ah sey, ah want it short,
Short back an' side,
Ah tell him man, ah tell him
When ah teck him aside,
Ah sey, ah want a haircut
Ah can wear with pride,
So lef' it long on top
But short back an' side.

Ah sey try an' put a pattern
In the shorter part,
Yuh could put a skull an' crossbone,
Or an arrow through a heart,
Meck sure ah have enough hair lef'
Fe cover me wart,
Lef a likkle pon the top,
But the res' – keep it short.

Well, bwoy, him start to cut
An' me settle down to wait,
Him was cuttin' from seven
Till half-past eight,
Ah was startin' to get worried
'cause ah see it gettin' late,
But then him put the scissors down
Sey 'There yuh are, mate.'

Well ah did see a skull an a
Criss-cross bone or two,
But was me own skull an bone
That was peepin' through
Ah look jus' like a monkey
Ah did see once at the zoo,
Him sey, 'What's de matter, Tammy,
Don't yuh like the hair-do?'

Well, ah feel me heart stop beatin'
When me look pon me reflection,
Ah feel like somet'ing frizzle up
Right in me middle section
Ah look aroun' fe somewhey
Ah could crawl into an' hide
The day ah mek me brother cut
Me hair short back an' side.

Valerie Bloom

Hush Hush

Norman is
a
secret agent.
Only family
and
close friends
know this.
Those of you
who have read
this poem
please
destroy it
and
forget
you ever
saw
it.

John C. Desmond

I Raised a Great Hullabaloo

I raised a great hullabaloo
When I found a large mouse in my stew,
Said the waiter, 'Don't shout
And wave it about,
Or the rest will be wanting one, too!'

Anon

The Bug Chant

Red bugs, bed bugs,
find them on your head bugs.

Green bugs, mean bugs,
lanky, long and lean bugs.

Pink bugs, sink bugs,
swimming in your drink bugs.

Yellow bugs, mellow bugs,
lazy little fellow bugs.

White bugs, night bugs,
buzzing round the light bugs.

Black bugs, slack bugs,
climbing up your back bugs.

Blue bugs, goo bugs,
find them in your shoe bugs.

Thin bugs, fat bugs,
hiding in your hat bugs.

Big bugs, small bugs,
crawling on your wall bugs.

Smooth bugs, hairy bugs,
flying like a fairy bugs.

Garden bugs, house bugs,
lumpy little louse bugs.

Fierce bugs, tame bugs,
some without a name bugs.

Far bugs, near bugs,
'What's this over here?' bugs.

Whine bugs, drone bugs,
write some of your own bugs.

Bzzzzzzzzzzzzzzzzz . . .

Tony Mitton

Team Talk

We're up against a team
that knows its onions –
not much about football.
It's the way they play
that makes you cry.

Including the sub.
It's the 'dirty dozen';
the shin-hackers, shirt-pullers
and elbow-diggers.

We are going to show them,
expose them for what they are,
embarrass them from the kick off,
unnerve them with new tactics
of very close marking.

As soon as the whistle blows
you turn to the nearest man
and pull his shorts down.

John C. Desmond

To Be or Not To Be

I sometimes think I'd rather crow
And be a rooster than to roost
And be a crow. But I dunno.

A rooster he can roost also,
Which don't seem fair when crows can't crow.
Which may help, some. Still I dunno.

Crows should be glad of one thing, though;
Nobody thinks of eating crow,
While roosters they are good enough
For anyone unless they're tough.

There are lots of tough old roosters though,
And anyway a crow can't crow,
So mebby roosters stand more show.
It looks that way. But I dunno.

Anon

It's Raining Cats and Dogs

It's raining cats and dogs –
The sky is growing dark,
Instead of pitter-patter
It's splatter, yowl and bark.

Bulldogs bounce on bonnets,
Alsatians hang in trees,
Poodles land on policemen
And bring them to their knees.

Tabby cats come squealing
Like rockets overhead,
Siamese look worried
At pavements turning red.

It's raining cats and dogs,
Although it shouldn't oughta.
Next time I pray for rain,
I'll add that I mean water.

Steve Turner

I Went to the Pictures Next Thursday

I went to the pictures next Thursday
I took a front seat at the back
I said to the lady behind me,
'I cannot see over your hat.'

She gave me some well-broken biscuits
I ate them and handed them back
I fell through a hole in the ceiling
and broke my breastbone in my back.

Anon

I Only Asked

On Sunday Dominic asked his Dad:
'Which is the brightest star?'
'Ask your Mum,' his Dad replied,
'I have to clean the car.'

On Monday Dominic asked his Mum:
'What's a carburettor?'
'Ask your Dad,' his Mum replied,
'I've got to post this letter.'

On Tuesday Dominic asked his Dad:
'What's a UFO?'
'Ask your Mum,' his Dad replied,
'The grass it needs a mow.'

On Wednesday Dominic asked his Mum:
'Which is the deepest sea?'
'Ask your Dad,' his Mum replied,
'I'm busy making tea.'

On Thursday Dominic asked his Dad:
'How tall are Kangaroos?'
'Ask your Mum,' his Dad replied.
'I'm listening to the news.'

On Friday Dominic asked his Dad:
'Do all kings have a crown?'
'Ask your Mum,' his Dad replied,
'I'm going into town.'

On Saturday Dominic asked them both:
'Do you mind me asking things,
About stars and cars and life on Mars
And Kangaroos and Kings?'

'Of course we don't,' his Dad replied,
'Ask questions as you grow.'
'By asking things,' his mother cried,
'That's how you get to know.'

Little Dominic scratched his head,
And simply answered, 'Oh!'

Gervase Phinn

A Stick Insect

A stick insect
is not a thick insect,
a macho-built-like-a-brick insect,
a brawl-and-break-it-up-quick insect,
not a sleek-and-slippery-slick insect
or a hold-out-your-hand-for-a-lick insect.

No way could you say it's a cuddly pet
or a butterfly that hasn't happened yet.

And it won't come running when you call
or chase about after a ball.
And you can't take it out for a walk
or try to teach it how to talk.

It's a hey-come-and-look-at-this-quick insect,
a how-can-you-tell-if-it's-sick insect,
a don't-mistake-me-for-a-stick
        insect . . .

Brian Moses

Michael Finnigin

There was an old man called Michael Fin-ni-gin,
He grew whiskers on his chin-i-gin,
The wind came up and blew them in-i-gin,
Poor old Mich-ael Fin-ni-gin. Be-gin-i-gin!

There was an old man called Michael Finnigin,
He kicked up an awful dinigin,
Because they said he must not sinigin,
Poor old Michael Finnigin. Beginigin!

There was an old man called Michael Finnigin,
He went fishing with a pinigin,
Caught a fish but dropped it inigin,
Poor old Michael Finnigin. Beginigin!

There was an old man called Michael Finnigin,
Climbed a tree and barked his shinigin,
Took off several yards of skinigin,
Poor old Michael Finnigin. Beginigin!

There was an old man called Michael Finnigin,
He grew fat and then grew thinigin,
Then he died and had to beginigin,
Poor old Michael Fin – ni – gin, STOP!

Anon

The Marrog

My desk's at the back of the class
And nobody, nobody knows
I'm a Marrog from Mars
With a body of brass
And seventeen fingers and toes.
Wouldn't they shriek if they knew
I've three eyes at the back of my head
And my hair is bright purple
My nose is deep blue
And my teeth are half-yellow, half-red?
My five arms are silver and spiked
With knives on them sharper than spears.
I could go back right now, if I liked –
And return in a million light-years.
I could gobble them all
For I'm seven foot tall
And I'm breathing green flames from my ears.
Wouldn't they yell if they knew,
If they guessed that a Marrog was here?
Ha-ha they haven't a clue –
Or wouldn't they tremble with fear!
'Look, look, a Marrog'
They'd all scream – and SMACK
The blackboard would fall and the ceiling would crack
And the teacher would faint, I suppose.
But I grin to myself, sitting right at the back
And nobody, nobody knows.

R. C. Scriven

The Elephant

When people call this beast to mind,
They marvel more and more
At such a *little* tail behind
So LARGE a trunk before.

Hilaire Belloc

Better Be Kind to Them Now

A squirrel is digging up the bulbs
In half the time Dad took to bury them.

A small dog is playing football
With a mob of boys. He beats them all,
Scoring goals at both ends.
A kangaroo would kick the boys as well.

Birds are so smart they can drink milk
Without removing the bottle-top.

Cats stay clean, and never have to be
Carried screaming to the bathroom.
They don't get their heads stuck in railings,
They negotiate first with their whiskers.

The gecko walks on the ceiling, and
The cheetah can outrun the Royal Scot.
The lion cures his wounds by licking them,
And the guppy has fifty babies at a go.

The cicada plays the fiddle for hours on end,
And a man-size flea could jump over St Paul's.

If ever these beasts should get together
Then we are done for, children.
I don't much fancy myself as a python's pet,
But it might come to that!

D. J. Enright

The Dream Keeper

Bring me all your dreams,
You dreamers,
Bring me all of your
Heart melodies
That I may wrap them
In a blue cloud-cloth
Away from the too-rough fingers
Of the world.

Langston Hughes

The Sleepy Giant

My age is three hundred and seventy-two,
And I think, with the deepest regret,
How I used to pick up and voraciously chew
The dear little boys whom I met.

I've eaten them raw, in their holiday suits;
I've eaten them curried with rice;
I've eaten them baked, in their jackets and boots,
And found them exceedingly nice.

But now that my jaws are weak for such fare,
I think it exceedingly rude
To do such a thing, when I'm quite well aware
Little boys do not like to be chewed.

And so I contentedly live upon eels,
And try to do nothing amiss,
And I pass all the time I can spare from my meals
In innocent slumber – like this.

Charles Edward Carryl

James and Mrs Curry

A carrot called James –
Yes, carrots have names –
Looked up from the veg patch and wondered
Why plump Mrs Curry
Seemed in such a hurry
As down through the garden she thundered.

Between the broad beans
And trembling greens
That shrank from her merciless stride,
She moved like an arrow
Past leek, sprout and marrow
To suddenly stop at James' side.

'I thought it looked fine,
That boiled beef of mine,
But no, it needs carrots,' she muttered,
'At least just the one,
Cooked briskly till done
To a turn and then lavishly buttered.'

With that she bent low
And, choosing James' row,
Grabbed hold of his feathery top,
To jump like a kitten
That thinks it's been bitten
When James cried out angrily: "Stop!

'Hands off or I'll thump you,
I'll batter you, bump you
And, struggling as hard as I'm able,
Put up a fierce fight
With all of my might
From here to the dining-room table!'

Poor woman; what squeals!
She took to her heels
And fled away, stammering: 'S-s-s-s-save me!'
And never, since then,
Served carrots again,
Just dunked soggy bread in her gravy.

Richard Edwards

The Frogs' History

You caught and carried us, pleased with yourselves.
We were only blobs of black in jars.

You knew what we'd become, were glad to wait.
How hectically we swam in that glass cage!

And there was never hope of an escape.
You put us on a shelf with more care than

You generally move. We were a hope,
A something-to-look-forward to, a change,

Almost a conjuring trick. Some sleight of nature
Would, given time, change us to your possessions.

We would be green and glossy, wet to touch.
'Take them away,' squeamish grown-ups would

Call out. Not you. You longed to hold us in
Your dry palms with surprising gentleness

And with a sense of unexpected justice
Would let us go, wanted to see us leap

And watch our eyes which never seem to sleep,
Hear our hideous but lively croak.

We know as well as you we are a joke.

Elizabeth Jennings

Divorce

I did not promise
to stay with you till death us do part, or
anything like that,
so part I must, and quickly. There are things
I cannot suffer
any longer: Mother, you have never, ever, said
a kind word
or a thank you for all the tedious chores I have done;
Father, your breath
smells like a camel's and gives me the hump;
all you ever say is:
'Are you off in the cream puff, Lady Muck?'
In this day and age?
I would be better off in an orphanage.
I want a divorce.
There are parents in the world whose faces turn
up to the light
who speak in a soft murmur of rivers
and never shout.
There are parents who stroke their children's cheeks
in the dead night
and sing in the colourful voices of rainbows,
red to blue.
These parents are not you. I never chose you.
You are rough and wild,
I don't want to be your child. All you do is shout
and that's not right.
I will file for divorce in the morning at first light.

Jackie Kay

Announcing the Guests at the Space Beasts' Party

'The Araspew from Bashergrannd'
'The Cakkaspoo from Danglebannd'
'The Eggisplosh from Ferrintole'
'The Gurglenosh from Hiccupole'
'The Inkiblag from Jupitickle'
'The Kellogclag from Lamandpickle'
'The Mighteemoose from Nosuchplace'
'The Orridjuice from Piggiface'
'The Quizziknutt from Radishratt'
'The Spattersplut from Trikkicatt'
'The Underpance from Verristrong'
'The Willidance from Xrayblong'
'The Yuckyspitt from Ziggersplitt'

Wes Magee

Temper Temper

He kicked it, he smacked it,
He got a stick and whacked it;
But no matter how much he attacked it,
He couldn't make it move.

He pulled at it, he tore at it,
He shouted and he swore at it;
But no matter how much he got sore at it,
He couldn't make it move.

So Dad left his car at the shops,
caught a bus home,
and was cross with us for the rest of the day.

Mike Jubb

two friends

lydia and shirley have
two pierced ears and
two bare ones
five pigtails
two pairs of sneakers
two berets
two smiles
one necklace
one bracelet
lots of stripes and
one good friendship

Nikki Giovanni

The Mistletoe Bough

The mistletoe hung in the castle hall,
The holly branch shone on the old oak wall;
And the baron's retainers were blithe and gay,
And keeping their Christmas holiday.
The baron beheld with a father's pride
His beautiful child, young Lovell's bride;
While she with her bright eyes seemed to be
The star of the goodly company.

'I'm weary of dancing now,' she cried;
'Here tarry a moment – I'll hide – I'll hide!
And, Lovell, be sure thou'rt first to trace
The clue to my secret lurking place.'
Away she ran – and her friends began
Each tower to search and each nook to scan;
And young Lovell cried, 'Oh where dost thou hide?
I'm lonesome without thee, my own dear bride.'
They sought her that night! and they sought
her next day!
And they sought her in vain when a week
passed away!
In the highest – the lowest – the loneliest spot,
Young Lovell sought wildly – but found her not.
And years flew by, and their grief at last
Was told as a sorrowful tale long past,
And when Lovell appeared, the children cried,
'See! the old man weeps for his fairy bride.'

At length an oak chest, that had long lain hid,
Was found in the castle – they raised the lid –
And a skeleton form lay mouldering there,
In the bridal wreath of that lady fair!
Oh! sad was her fate! – in sportive jest
She hid from her lord in the old oak chest.
It closed with a spring! and, dreadful doom,
Thc bride lay clasped in her living tomb!

Thomas Haynes Bayly

Rover

for David Ross

I have a pet oyster called Rover.
He lives in the bathroom sink
and is never any trouble:
no birdseed or tins of Kennomeat,
no cat-litter.
We don't need to take him for walks,
we don't need an oyster-flap in the back door.

He doesn't bark
or sing,
just lies in the sink
and never says a thing.
Sometimes
when he feels irritable,
he grits his teeth
and produces a little pearl.

At night,
we tuck him up snug in his oyster-bed
until the bathroom tide comes in
in the morning.
Sometimes
I look at Rover and say,
'The world's your lobster,
Rover', I say.

Adrian Henri

Blood-Brothers

We're the best of friends.
We're pals for good.
We're blood-brothers, but
We don't like blood.
So, as tomatoes are just as red,
We're ketchup-brothers instead.

Celia Warren

The Broomstick Train

Look out! Look out, boys! Clear the track!
The witches are here! They've all come back!
They hanged them high. No use! No use!
What cares a witch for the hangman's noose?
They buried them deep, but they wouldn't lie still,
For cats and witches are hard to kill;
They swore they shouldn't and wouldn't die –
Books said they did, but they lie! they lie!

Oliver Wendell Holmes

A Ballad of John Silver

We were schooner-rigged and rakish, with a long
and lissome hull,
And we flew the pretty colours of the cross-bones
and the skull;
We'd a big black Jolly Roger flapping grimly at
the fore,
And we sailed the Spanish Water in the happy days
of yore.

We'd a long brass gun amidships, like a well-
conducted ship,
We had each a brace of pistols and a cutlass at
the hip;
It's a point which tells against us, and a fact to
be deplored,
But we chased the goodly merchantmen and laid their
ships aboard.

Then the dead men fouled the scuppers and the
wounded filled the chains,
And the paintwork all was spatter-dashed with
other people's brains,
She was boarded, she was looted, she was scuttled
till she sank.
And the pale survivors left us by the medium of
the plank.

O! then it was (while standing by the taffrail on
the poop)
We could hear the drowning folk lament the absent
chicken-coop;
Then, having washed the blood away, we'd little
else to do
Than to dance a quiet hornpipe as the old salts
taught us to.

O! the fiddle on the fo'c's'le, and the slapping naked
soles,
And the genial 'Down the middle, Jake, and curtsey
when she rolls'
With the silver seas around us and the pale moon
overhead,
And the look-out not a-looking and his pipe-bowl
glowing red.

Ah! the pig-tailed, quidding pirates and the pretty
pranks we played,
All have since been put a stop-to by the naughty
Board of Trade;
The schooners and the merry crews were laid
away to rest,
A little south the sunset in the Islands of the Blest.

John Masefield

Insides

I'm very grateful to my skin
For keeping all my insides in –
I do so hate to think about
What I would look like inside-out.

Colin West

Breakfast

I C U 8 your scrambled X,
I C U drank your T.
My heart is filled with NV,
R there NE X 4 me?
O Y is the carton MT now?
How greedy can U B?
4 U 8 all the scrambled X
And left me 1 green P!

Jeff Moss

Elephant Rules

Never be silly or mean
To an elephant,
Never feed chilli or beans
To an elephant,
Never go near
To the front or the rear
Of a chilliful, bellyful
Smellyphant.

David L. Harrison

The Meadow Mouse

I

In a shoe box stuffed in an old nylon stocking
Sleeps the baby mouse I found in the meadow,
Where he trembled and shook beneath a stick
Till I caught him up by the tail and brought him in,
Cradled in my hand,
A little quaker, the whole body of him trembling,
His absurd whiskers sticking out like a cartoon-mouse,
His feet like small leaves,
Little lizard-feet,
Whitish and spread wide when he tried to struggle away,
Wriggling like a minuscule puppy.

Now he's eaten his three kinds of cheese and drunk from
        his bottle-cap watering-trough –
So much he just lies in one corner,
His tail curled under him, his belly big
As his head, his bat-like ears
Twitching, tilting toward the least sound.

Do I imagine he no longer trembles
When I come close to him?
He seems no longer to tremble.

II

But this morning the shoe-box house on the back
porch is empty.
Where has he gone, my meadow mouse,
My thumb of a child that nuzzled in my palm? –
To run under the hawk's wing,
Under the eye of the great owl watching from
the elm-tree,
To live by courtesy of the shrike, the snake,
the tom-cat.

I think of the nestling fallen into the deep grass,
The turtle gasping in the dusty rubble of the highway,
The paralytic stunned in the tub, and the water rising, –
All things innocent, hapless, forsaken.

Theodore Roethke

Is Your Mum Like This?

My mum
wears
Deely-boppers
Silver-spangled tights
Tank tops
CND earrings
Bunches
An eye-patch
Fifteen bangles
(on each arm)
Leg-warmers
Platforms
Ra-ra skirts and flares
(together at the same time)
A monocle
Pom-poms
Headphones
Fingerless gloves
A top hat
and tails
And that's just
To go shopping.

Jane Wright

Chameleons

Chameleons are seldom seen,
They're red, they're orange, then they're green.
They're one of nature's strangest sights,
Their colours change like traffic lights!

Colin West

Who Made a Mess?

Who made a mess of the planet
And what's that bad smell in the breeze?
Who punched a hole in the ozone
And who took an axe to my trees?

Who sprayed the garden with poison
While trying to scare off a fly?
Who streaked the water with oil slicks
And who let my fish choke and die?

Who tossed that junk in the river
And who stained the fresh air with fumes?
Who tore the fields with a digger
And who blocked my favourite views?

Who's going to tidy up later
And who's going to find what you've lost?
Who's going to say that they're sorry
And who's going to carry the cost?

Steve Turner

Newborn Child

I am not a Buddhist,
I am not a Hindu,
I am not a Muslim –
but I'm just like you.

Just like you –
and you're just like me,
inside there are no differences
for us to see.

I am not a Christian,
I am not a Jew,
I am not a Heathen –
but I'm just like you.

Just like you –
and you're just like me,
and there isn't any simpler way
for us to be.

Norman Silver

Nature Made the Alligator

Longer, leaner, lighter, straighter,
nature made the alligator.

Underwater navigator,
denizen of the Equator,
bed of reeds or muddy crater.

Longer, leaner, lighter, straighter,
nature made the alligator.

Made its greed grow even greater,
predatory, patient waiter,
sneaky, silent prey-locator.

Longer, leaner, lighter, straighter,
nature made the alligator.

Cool and crafty calculator,
cruel and creeping infiltrator,
sudden-action operator.

Longer, leaner, lighter, straighter,
nature made the alligator.

Animal de-animator,
river-bank de-populator,
fish-farm thief and devastator.

Longer, leaner, lighter, straighter,
nature made the alligator.

Nick Toczek

Legs of my Uncles

Uncle John's are short,
Uncle Stan's are hairy,
Uncle Jim's are long,
Uncle Frank's are scary.

Ian McMillan and
Andrew McMillan

Mother Doesn't Want a Dog

Mother doesn't want a dog.
Mother says they smell,
And never sit when you say sit,
Or even when you yell.
And when you come home late at night
And there is ice and snow,
You have to go back out because
The dumb dog has to go.

Mother doesn't want a dog.
Mother says they shed,
And always let the strangers in
And bark at friends instead,
And do disgraceful things on rugs,
And track mud on the floor,
And flop upon your bed at night
And snore their doggy snore.

Mother doesn't want a dog.
She's making a mistake.
Because, more than a dog, I think
She will not want this snake.

Judith Viorst

Robin Hood

Robin Hood
Was an outlawed earl
He took to the wood
With a lovely girl,
And there and then
They were lord and queen
Of a band of men
In Lincoln green –
There was Scarlet Will, and Alan a Dale,
And great big Little John-O,
And Friar Tuck, that fat old buck,
And Much the Miller's son-O!

Robin Hood
He robbed the rich
And gave to the good
And needy, which,
When the moon was bright
And the sport was rare,
Seemed only right
And fair and square
To Scarlet Will, and Alan a Dale,
And great big Little John-O,
And Friar Tuck, that fat old buck,
And Much the Miller's son-O!

Robin Hood
He poached the deer
And moistened his food
With stolen beer –
Hark how they sing
And shout and flout
The knavish king
Who turned him out
With Scarlet Will, and Alan a Dale,
And great big Little John-O,
And Friar Tuck, that fat old buck,
And Much the Miller's son-O!

Eleanor Farjeon

Cake-Face

I like chocolate
cake, I like birthday
cake, I like ginger
cake, I like sponge
cake, I like fruit
cake, I like Christmas
cake, I like carrot
cake, I just can't stand
stoma
cake.

David Horner

Food for Thought

Slugs that slither near your mushrooms
Have a tendency to hide.
Look out when you take a mouthful,
Those chewier bits are soft inside.

Flies that settle on your biscuit
Stay so still and blend right in.
Look out for the bits that tickle
Just as you are swallowing.

Worms that wander near spaghetti
Lose their footing and fall in.
Look out, for that bit you're sucking
Look as if it's wriggling.

If you sneeze when near green chutney
Have the goodness to confess,
Suspicious lumps and slimy green bits
Could occasion some distress.

If you're offered Irish stew
With meat and veg chunks brown and thick,
It might be kinder not to mention
That the dog has just been sick.

Michaela Morgan

Dream Team

My team
Will have all the people in it
Who're normally picked last.

Such as me.

When it's my turn to be chooser
I'll overlook Nick Magic-Feet Jones
And Supersonic Simon Hughes

And I'll point at my best friend Sean
Who'll faint with surprise
And delight.

And at Robin who's always the one
Left at the end that no one chose –
Unless he's away, in which case it's guess who?

And Tim who can't see a thing
Without his glasses.
I'll pick him.

And the rest of the guys that Mr Miller
Calls dead-legs but only need their chance
To show what they're made of.

We'll play in the cup final
In front of the class, the school, the town,
The world, the galaxy.

And due to the masterly leadership shown
By their captain, not forgetting
His three out-of-this-world goals,

We'll WIN.

Frances Nagle

Sister Sounds

I can't understand it,
Can you?
But it's true
That whales are enormous.
Yet they speak
With a tiny squeal
And a gentle squeak.
But my sister,
Who's only two,
Makes the most awful
Hullabaloo.

I can't understand it,
Can you?

Max Fatchen

Witch

There was this old lady on the bus . . .
	(Old cat! Sourpuss!)
Gave her my hand to pull her on.
'OK, love . . . let me help you, Gran.'
But she hissed and spat like a real old mog . . .
Eye of newt and toe of frog.
(She wasn't a bit like my old Nan
Who smells of cake and apple jam.)
If she'd lived two hundred years ago
They'd have ducked her for a witch, you know.

But then I thought . . .   If her life's been rough,
Why – that's enough
To make her tough . . .
. . . and spitefulhard.
You never can really tell, you see –
In sixty years that might be me.

Marion Lines

Instructions for Giants

Please do not step on swing parks, youth clubs,
 cinemas or discos.
Please flatten all schools!

Please do not eat children, pop stars, TV soap actors,
 kind grannies who give us 50p.
Please feel free to gobble up dentists and teachers
 any time you like!

Please do not block out the sunshine.
Please push all rain clouds over to France.

Please do not drink the public swimming pool.
Please eat all cabbage fields, vegetable plots
and anything green that grows in the
 boring countryside!

Please do not trample kittens, lambs or other baby
 animals.
Please take spiders and snakes, ants and beetles home
 for your own pets.

Please stand clear of jets passing.
Please sew up the ozone layer.
Please mind where you're putting your big feet –
and no sneaking off to China when we're playing
 hide-and-seek!

John Rice

Song in Space

When man first flew beyond the sky
He looked back into the world's blue eye.
Man said: What makes your eye so blue?
Earth said: The tears in the ocean do.
Why are the seas so full of tears?
Because I've wept so many thousand years.
Why do you weep as you dance through space?
Because I am the mother of the human race.

Adrian Mitchell

Get Your Things Together, Hayley

Mum said the dreaded words this morning,
'Get your things together, Hayley,
We're moving.'

I've at last made a friend, and Mrs Gray
Has just stopped calling me
The New Girl.

Why do we have to go now
When I'm just beginning
To belong?

It's OK for my sister,
She's good with people.
They like her.

But I can't face the thought
Of starting all over again,
In the wrong uniform,

Knowing the wrong things,
In a class full of strangers
Who've palled up already

And don't need me.
Mum says, 'It's character-forming, Hayley.'
I say it's terribly lonely.

Frances Nagle

The King sent for his wise men all
    To find a rhyme for W.
When they had thought a good long time
But could not think of a single rhyme,
    'I'm sorry,' said he, 'to trouble you.'

James Reeves

Dear Mum,

While you were out
a cup went and broke itself,
a crack appeared in the blue vase
your great-great grandad
brought back from Mr Ming in China.
Somehow, without me even turning on the tap,
the sink mysteriously overflowed.
A strange jam-stain,
about the size of a boy's hand,
appeared on the kitchen wall.
I don't think we will ever discover
exactly how the cat
managed to turn on the washing-machine
(specially from the inside),
or how Sis's pet rabbit went and mistook
the waste-disposal unit for a burrow.
I can tell you I was scared when,
as if by magic,
a series of muddy footprints
appeared on the new white carpet.
I was being good
(honest)
but I think the house is haunted so,
knowing you're going to have a fit,
I've gone over to Gran's for a bit.

Brian Patten

Centrifugalized in Finsbury Park

Hey I just had a go on one of them
things! Didn't notice it had a name,
but anyone could see what it was going to do to you –

something like a giant-size round biscuit-tin without
a lid
made of wire-netting, and all around the inside,
niches, like for statues, 30 or so, like coffins, only
upright, and open of course with the kind of lattice –
with a padded red heart at head-height.

Paid the money, got myself a niche, and stood
and waited
with a little chain dangling across my hips,
until it was full, the gate shut, the music started
and the thing began to whirl.

It wasn't the stomach, it was what to do with the head:
no good looking down, but if you let your head back
it felt as if it was going to go on going back, or off –
a bit peculiar, shut my eyes to get through that.

And as it whirled, the whole thing turned on end,
more or less vertical – well, I'd seen that right from
the park gates and couldn't believe it, which was why –
and opening my eyes again then, just found myself
lying there – lying down face up, lying up face down
over the whole fairground!

And it didn't make you scream like the top of the Big
Wheel, but smile – look up and everyone else is
  standing there,
hanging there, smiling, look down and you might as
  well be a lazy
bird on the wind, though I did forget I could let go,

and the only strange feeling was,
every time you were on the down side hurtling
  up again,
you left the skin of your face behind for a second.
You know I've never dared try anything quite like that
before, and it was just very nice!

And when it slowed down and sank down, and all of us
were ordinary upright, and unhitched our little chains,
I only staggered a couple of times, disappearing
on ground level into the dark – and nobody was sick.

Libby Houston

Monster of Slob

My room's a mess, an awful mess.
What all is here, I just can't guess.
Mildewed towels and muddy shoes,
Paints and paste I never use.
Banana peels and wads of gum,
A rusty old aquarium.
Dirty socks and Tuesday's snack,
A suitcase that I should unpack.
No place to stand, no place to sit –
Say – isn't that pile shifting a bit?
Isn't it moving closer to me?
Is that a pair of eyes I see?
Is that an arm that's reaching out?
Is that a claw? Is that a snout?
I see its face, and now I see
it's really coming after me.
I should have listened when Mom said
to clean my room and make my bed.
My mess has changed, I don't know how.
It's turned into a monster now.
I march that monster out the door
and follow it outside.
I watch it as it lumbers off . . .
It turns to wave goodbye.

The mess is gone.
My room is clean.
My parents will be glad.
But me, I really miss my mess –
the best I've ever had.

If I start now
and work real fast,
I can get it done:
I'll start a new mess right away –
a bigger, better one!

Florence Parry Heide and Roxanne Heide Pierce

Mossie

Don't ya mess wi me, pal,
my aim is true.
Stiletto in the shadows
hunting for you.

Nip ya on the finger,
armpit, neck or knee;
Jag ya anywhur ah like,
ya can't stop me.

See them mobbing midgies,
gang a mugging fleas;
Na style, na class, just numbers,
there's none as brave as me.

Wasps are dumb and clumsy,
one stroke an they're dud,
they're just easily upset
but I'm out for your blood.

Sandflies are sneaky nippers –
I'm elegant and proud;
Hear me coming, human,
I'll be singing clear and loud.

I like to boast and dance around
before I get stuck in –
when you can't hear me then fear
cos I'll be sucking skin.

'Float like a butterfly,
Sting like a bee' –
man, I can do all that an' more,
you've no chance against me!

Dave Calder

Three Wise Men of Gotham

Three wise men of Gotham,
They went to sea in a bowl,
And if the bowl had been stronger
My song would be longer.

Anon

Be Careful of Cousins

When cousin Jeremy was one
He crawled into a drain for fun.

When cousin Jeremy was two
He did the things you shouldn't do.

When cousin Jeremy was three
He poured the cat's milk in the tea.

When Jeremy was barely four
I didn't like him any more.

At five he played such awful tricks
Which lasted till the age of six.

From seven, until nearly eight,
Our mother said he tempted fate
Especially when at naughty nine
He pegged my sister on the line.

This ghastly news I now must pen,
Tomorrow JEREMY IS TEN!

Max Fatchen

Do Not Spit

There was an old man of Darjeeling
Who travelled from London to Ealing
It said on the door,
'Please don't spit on the floor,'
So he carefully spat on the ceiling.

Anon

In Between

My sister goes to the movies
My brother stays home in his crib.
I'm too young to go with my sister
And too old for wearing a bib.
Too grown-up to be baby-sat for,
But too young to go baby-sit.
So if there's one age that is lousy,
I'll tell you for sure this is it.

Jeff Moss

The Common Cormorant

The common cormorant or shag
Lays eggs inside a paper bag.
The reason you will see no doubt
It is to keep the lightning out.
But what these unobservant birds
Have never noticed is that herds
Of wandering bears may come with buns
And steal the bags to hold the crumbs.

Anon

All But Blind

All but blind
    In his chambered hole
Gropes for worms
    The four-clawed Mole.

All but blind
    In the evening sky
The hooded Bat
    Twirls softly by.

All but blind
    In the burning day
The Barn Owl blunders
    On her way.

And blind as are
    These three to me,
So, blind to Some-One
    I must be.

Walter de la Mare

It's Dark in Here

I am writing these lines
From inside a lion,
And it's rather dark in here.
So please excuse the handwriting
Which may not be too clear.
But this afternoon by the lion's cage
I'm afraid I got too near.
And I'm writing these lines
From inside a lion,
And it's rather dark in here.

Shel Silverstein

Walking the Dog Seems Like Fun to Me

I said, The dog wants a walk.

Mum said to Dad, It's your turn.
Dad said, I always walk the dog.
Mum said, Well I walked her this morning.
Dad said, She's your dog –
I didn't want a dog in the first place.

Mum said, It's your turn.

Dad stood up and threw the remote control
at the pot plant.
Dad said, I'm going down the pub.
Mum said, Take the dog.

Dad shouted, No way!
Mum shouted, You're going nowhere!

I grabbed Judy's lead
and we both bolted out the back door.

The stars were shining like diamonds.
Judy sniffed at a hedgehog, rolled up in a ball.
She ate a discarded kebab on the pavement.
She chased a cat that ran up a tree.

Walking the dog
seems like fun to me.

Roger Stevens

This Kissing Business

Should I part my lips, or pucker?
Bite them tightly? Blow or suck or

hold my breath? Perhaps I'll practise
on my mirror. See, the fact is

I'm not sure what is expected
when four lips become connected.

Gina Douthwaite

The Joke

The joke you just told isn't funny one bit.
It's pointless and dull, wholly lacking in wit.
It's old and stale, it's beginning to smell!
Besides, it's the one I was going to tell.

Anon

Walls

Walls are quite useful,
Here is what they're for:
Walls keep your ceiling
From falling on your floor.

Jeff Moss

Witches' Chant

Round about the cauldron go:
In the poisoned entrails throw.
Toad, that under cold stone
Days and nights has thirty-one
Sweated venom sleeping got,
Boil thou first in the charmèd pot.
    Double, double toil and trouble;
    Fire burn and cauldron bubble.

Fillet of a fenny snake,
In the cauldron boil and bake;
Eye of newt and toe of frog,
Wool of bat and tongue of dog,
Adder's fork and blindworm's sting,
Lizard's leg and owlet's wing.
For a charm of powerful trouble,
Like a hell-broth boil and bubble.
    Double, double toil and trouble;
    Fire burn and cauldron bubble.

Scale of dragon, tooth of wolf,
Witch's mummy, maw and gulf
Of the ravenous salt-sea shark,
Root of hemlock digged in the dark,
Make the gruel thick and slab:
Add thereto a tiger's chaudron,
For the ingredients of our cauldron.
    Double, double toil and trouble,
    Fire burn and cauldron bubble.

William Shakespeare
(from *Macbeth*)

Acknowledgements

The compiler and publishers wish to thank the following for permission to use copyright material:

John Agard, 'A Date With Spring' from *Get Back Pimple* by John Agard, Viking (1996), by permission of Caroline Sheldon Literary Agency on behalf of the author; **Hilaire Belloc**, 'The Elephant' from *Cautionary Verses* by Hilaire Belloc, Random House UK. Copyright © The Estate of Hilaire Belloc, by permission of Peters Fraser and Dunlop on behalf of the Estate of the author; **James Berry**, 'The Barkday Party' from *When I Dance* by James Berry, Hamish Hamilton Children's Books. Copyright © James Berry, by permission of Peters Fraser and Dunlop on behalf of the author; **Valerie Bloom**, 'Haircut Rap' from *Let Me Touch the Sky*, Macmillan Children's Books (2000), by permission of the author; **Phil Bolsta**, 'The Toothless Wonder' from *Kids Pick the Funniest Poems*, ed. Bruce Lansky. Copyright © 1991 by Phil Bolsta, by permission of Meadowbrook Press; **Dave Calder**, 'Mossie', by permission of the author; **Charles Causley**, 'I Want to be Monday' from *Collected Poems for Children* by Charles Causley, Macmillan, by permission of David Higham Associates on behalf of the author; **John Coldwell**, 'A Poem With Two Lauras In It' from *Custard Pie*, ed. Pie Corbett, Macmillan (1996), by permission of the author; **John Desmond**, 'Team Talk' and 'Hush, Hush', by permission of the author; **Peter Dixon**, 'Lone Mission' from *Peter Dixon's Grand Prix of Poetry*, Macmillan, by permission of the author; **Lord Alfred Douglas**, 'The Hen', by permission of Sheila Colman on behalf of the Estate of the author; **Gina Douthwaite**, 'This Kissing Business'. Copyright © Gina Douthwaite, by permission of the author; **Richard Edwards**, 'The Word Party' and 'James and Mrs Curry', by permission of the author; **D. J. Enright**, 'Better Be Kind To Them Now', Oxford University Press, by permission of Watson, Little Ltd on behalf of the author; **Eleanor Farjeon and Herbert Farjeon**, 'Robin Hood' from *Heroes and Heroines* by Eleanor Farjeon and Herbert Farjeon, J M Dent, by permission of David Higham Associates on behalf of the authors; **Max Fatchen**, 'Sister Sounds' and 'Be Careful of Cousins' from *Peculiar Rhymes and Lunatic Lines* by Max Fatchen, Orchard Books (1995), by permission of The Watts Publishing Group Ltd; **David L. Harrison**, 'Elephant Rules' from *The Boy Who Counted Stars* by David L. Harrison, Wordsong Boyd Mills Press (1994), by permission of the author; **Trevor Harvey**, 'The Painting Lesson' first published in *Funny Poems*, Usborne (1990), by permission of the author; **Florence Parry Heide and Roxanne Heide Pierce**, 'Monster of Slob', first published in *Oh, Grow Up!*, Orchard Books. Copyright © 1996 by Florence Parry Heide and Roxanne Heide Pierce, by permission of Orchard Books, New York and Curtis Brown, Ltd on behalf of the authors; **Adrian Henri**, 'Rover' from *Rhinestone Rhino and Other Poems* by Adrian Henri, Methuen. Copyright © Adrian Henri 1989, by permission of Rogers Coleridge and

White on behalf of the author; **David Horner**, 'Cake-Face', by permission of the author; **Libby Houston**, 'Centrifugalized in Finsbury Park' from *Cover of Darkness, Selected Poems 1961-1998*, Slow Dancer Press (1991, 1999). Copyright © Libby Houston 1991, by permission of the author; **Langston Hughes**, 'The Dream Keeper' from *Collected Poems* by Langston Hughes. Copyright © 1994 by the Estate of Langston Hughes, by permission of Alfred A. Knopf, a division of Random House, Inc and David Higham Associates on behalf of the Estate of the author; **Elizabeth Jennings**, 'The Frog's History' from *Collected Poems* by Elizabeth Jennings, Carcanet Press, by permission of David Higham Associates on behalf of the author; **Mike Jubb**, 'Temper Temper'. Copyright © Mike Jubb, by permission of the author; **Jackie Kay**, 'The Want-Want Twins' and 'Divorce', by permission of the author; **Marian A. Lines**, 'Witch' from *Tower Blocks* by Marian A. Lines, by permission of the author; **Roger McGough**, 'The Missing Sock' from *Pillow Talk*, Viking Penguin. Copyright © 1990 Roger McGough, by permission of Peters Fraser & Dunlop Group Ltd on behalf of the author; **Ian McMillan**, 'Ready Salted'; and with **Andrew McMillan**, 'Legs of My Uncles', by permission of the authors; **Lindsay MacRae**, '2 Poems about 4 Eyes' from *You Canny Shove Yer Granny off a Bus!*, Viking. Copyright © Lindsay MacRae, 1995, by permission of The Agency (London) Ltd on behalf of the author; **Wes Magee**, 'At the End of a School Day' and 'Announcing the guests at the Space Beasts Party'. Copyright © Wes Magee, by permission of the author; **Walter de la Mare**, 'All but Blind' from *The Complete Poems of Walter de la Mare*, by permission of the Society of Authors as representative of the Literary Trustees of the author; **John Masefield**, 'Ballad of John Silver', by permission of the Society of Authors as representative of the Estate of the author; **Adrian Mitchell**, 'Song in Space' from *Adrian Mitchell's Greatest Hits*, Bloodaxe Books (1991) Copyright © 1991 Adrian Mitchell, by permission of Peters Fraser and Dunlop on behalf of the author; **Tony Mitton**, 'The Bug Chant'. Copyright © Tony Mitton 1998, by permission of the author; **Lilian Moore**, 'Until I Saw the Sea' from *I Feel the Same Way* by Lilian Moore. Copyright © 1967, 1995 Lilian Moore, by permission of Marian Reiner on behalf of the author; **Michaela Morgan**, 'Food for Thought', by permission of the author; **Brian Moses**, 'Stick Insect', by permission of the author; **Jeff Moss**, 'Breakfast', 'Walls' and 'In Between' from *The Other Side of the Door* by Jeff Moss. Copyright © 1991 by Jeff Moss, by permission of Bantam Books, a division of Random House, Inc and ICM, Inc on behalf of the author; **Frances Nagle**, 'Dream Team' and 'Get Your Things Together, Hayley' from *You can't call a hedgehog Hopscotch* by Frances Nagle, Dagger Press (1999), by permission of the author; **Brian Patten**, 'Dear Mum' from *Thawing Frozen Frogs* by Brian Patten, Viking. Copyright © Brian Patten 1990, by permission of Rogers Coleridge and White on behalf of the author; **Simon Pitt**, 'The Sleepy Goalie', by permission of the author; **James Reeves**, 'W' from *Complete Poems for Children* by James Reeves, Heinemann. Copyright © James Reeves, by permission of Laura Cecil Literary Agency on behalf of the Estate of the author; **John Rice**, 'Instructions for Giants', by permission of the author;

Theodore Roethke, 'The Meadow Mouse' from *Collected Poems of Theodore Roethke.* Copyright © 1963 by Beatrice Roethke, Administratrix of the Estate of Theodore Roethke, by permission of Faber and Faber Ltd and Doubleday, a division of Random House, Inc; **Vernon Scannell**, 'Death of a Snowman', by permission of the author; **R. C. Scriven**, 'The Marrog', by permission of Marc Scriven; **Ian Serraillier**, 'The Visitor', by permission of Anne Serraillier; **Norman Silver**, 'Newborn Child' from *The Walkmen Have Landed*, Faber and Faber (1994). Copyright © Norman Silver 1994, by permission of Laura Cecil Literary Agency on behalf of the author; **Shel Silverstein**, 'It's Dark in Here' from *Where the Sidewalk Ends* by Shel Silverstein. Copyright © 1974 by Evil Eye Music, Inc, by permission of HarperCollins Publishers, Inc and Edite Kroll Literary Agency on behalf of the author; **Roger Stevens**, 'Walking The Dog Seems Like Fun To Me' and 'Mobile Home For Sale', by permission of the author; **Nick Toczek**, 'Nature Made the Alligator', by permission of the author; **Steve Turner**, 'Who Made A Mess' and 'It's Raining Cats and Dogs' from *The Day I Fell Down The Toilet*, by permission of Lion Publishing PLC; **Judith Viorst**, 'Mother Doesn't Want a Dog' from *If I Were in Charge of the World and Other Worries* by Judith Viorst. Copyright © 1981 Judith Viorst, by permission of Atheneum Books for Young Readers, an imprint of Simon & Schuster Children's Publishing Division and A M Heath & Co Ltd on behalf of the author; **Barrie Wade**, 'Studup', by permission of the author; **Celia Warren**, 'Blood-Brothers', by permission of the author; **Colin West**, 'Insides' and 'Chameleons', by permission of the author; **Jane Wright**, 'Is Your Mum Like This?', by permission of the author; **Kit Wright**, 'The Man Who Invented Football', by permission of the author.

Every effort has been made to trace the copyright holders but if any have been inadvertently overlooked the publishers will be pleased to make the necessary arrangement at the first opportunity.